The GOLF W.I.Z. Trivia Quiz

by Steve Heldt

RED-LETTER PRESS, INC.

THE GOLF WIZ TRIVIA QUIZ
Copyright ©2001 Red-Letter Press, Inc.
ISBN: 0-940462-52-4
All Rights Reserved
Printed in the United States of America

For information address:

Red-Letter Press, Inc.
P.O. Box 393, Saddle River, NJ 07458

ACKNOWLEDGMENTS

Cover design
and typography: s.w.artz, inc.

Editorial: Ellen Fischbein

Contributors: Angela Demers
Jack Kreismer

INTRODUCTION

Red-Letter Press proudly tees up
The Golf Wiz Trivia Quiz. Formatted in ten-
question quizzes, it features an all-star selection
of stumpers for the nineteenth hole.

Steve Heldt brings you a book loaded with
trivia ... What's a *muni*? ... Of all the players to
win a major title, who comes first alphabetically?
... Who holds the dubious distinction of playing
in the most Masters without winning any?

The answers are all inside. Now let's find out
if you're a golf wiz or a wannabe.

Jack Kreismer
Publisher

TEEING OFF

Here's a quiz designed to get you off to a good start,
without having to use a mulligan.

1. By the way, what is a *mulligan*?

2. To what do the initials, USGA, refer?

3. Par for the hole is four, and I shoot a three. What is my
   score called?

4. Name the only Grand Slam event played on foreign soil.

5. What player is awarded the Vardon Trophy each year?

6. What country does Jesper Parnevik call home?

7. It's the only major played in April. Name it.

8. What's the minimum age a golfer must be to play on the
   Senior PGA Tour?

9. How many clubs are you allowed to carry in your bag during
   a match, twelve or fourteen?

10. True or false? Lee Trevino won two Masters championships.

CHIP SHOTS

"At first I said, 'Let's play for taxes.'"

*–Michael Jordan, when asked about
playing a round with President Clinton*

ANSWERS

1. A second shot, usually off the first tee, that is sometimes permitted in a casual game, but never in a competition played strictly by the *Rules of Golf*

2. The United States Golf Association

3. A birdie

4. The British Open

5. The PGA member who has the best scoring average on the Tour that year

6. Sweden

7. The Masters is played the second weekend in April.

8. One has to be at least fifty years old.

9. Fourteen

10. False — Trevino never won The Masters.

CHIP SHOTS

"I find it to be the hole-in-one."

–Groucho Marx, on golf's toughest shot

GOING OUT

Name the golf courses described below.

1. The Masters is played here.

2. Its 17th hole is called the Road Hole.

3. Site of the 1999 Ryder Cup

4. Permanent host of the Tournament Players Championship, it's known for its island green at the 17th hole.

5. The first clubhouse in America opened here in 1892.

6. The South Carolina course which was awarded a Ryder Cup before it was completed

7. The public course at which Tom Watson won his U.S. Open in 1982

8. The course where the United States lost the Ryder Cup for the first time on American soil

9. It's where Bobby Jones capped off his Grand Slam with a win in the U.S. Amateur.

10. At 107 yards, its 7th hole is the shortest in the history of the majors.

ANSWERS

1. Augusta National
2. The Old Course at St. Andrews
3. The Country Club at Brookline, MA
4. The Tournament Players Club at Sawgrass
5. Shinnecock Hills in Southhampton, NY
6. The Ocean Course at Kiawah Island
7. Pebble Beach
8. Muirfield Village in Dublin, OH
9. Merion Country Club
10. Pebble Beach

Chip Shots

"Don't blame me. Blame the foursome ahead of me."

–Pro football Hall of Famer Lawrence Taylor, on why he was late for practice

JOINING ARNIE'S ARMY

How much do you know about Arnold Palmer?

1. His father was the pro at this club which, to this day, remains Arnold's home course. Name it.

2. What year did Palmer become the first golfer to eclipse $100,000 in earnings in a single season?

3. In what branch of the military did the "general" of Arnie's Army serve?

4. True or false? Palmer won at least one PGA Tour event each year for seventeen straight years.

5. What course was the site of Palmer's only U.S. Open victory?

6. What was Palmer's last win on the regular PGA Tour?

7. Where did Arnie play his college golf?

8. What PGA Tour player receives the Palmer Trophy?

9. Palmer was honored by *Sports Illustrated* as its Sportsman of the Year in:
   A) 1955 B) 1960 C) 1965 D) 1970

10. Quick! Arnold's wife's name is ...

ANSWERS

1. The Latrobe Country Club in Latrobe, PA

2. Palmer won $128,230 in 1963.

3. Arnie served three years in the Coast Guard in the early '50s.

4. True — Palmer won one event every year from 1955 to 1971.

5. The Cherry Hill Country Club in Denver, CO

6. In 1973, Palmer won the Bob Hope Desert Classic.

7. Wake Forest University

8. The Tour's leading money winner for the year

9. B

10. Winifred

Chip Shots

"I don't even drive that far when I go on vacation."

–Raymond Floyd, on John Daly's driving prowess

FRIED EGGS AND UNPLAYABLE LIES

If these golfers didn't have any bad luck,
they wouldn't have had any luck at all. Can you name them?

1. His unfortunate legacy will be as the man who signed an incorrect scorecard at the 1968 Masters.

2. That mental block is not just a male thing. She was low scorer at the 1957 U.S. Women's Open, but signed an incorrect scorecard.

3. He has the dubious distinction of playing in The Masters the most times without winning it.

4. Lee Trevino, Jerry Heard and Bobby Nichols were struck by lightning at the 1975 Western Open. Only one of the three golfers was able to finish his round. Which one?

5. He scored a 23 on the 17th hole during the 1927 Shawnee Open, a record for one hole in an event.

6. In 1986, he was disqualified from both the Phoenix Open and the L.A. Open for hitting someone else's ball.

7. These two golfers can say that they've lost all four majors in playoffs.

8. He was disqualified from the 1980 U.S. Open after a traffic tie-up caused him to miss his tee time.

9. The first time instant replay was used in a tournament, he lost a stroke when videotape showed that a tee shot into the water should have been replayed from the tee, not a penalty drop.

10. This president was on the golf course in 1915 when he was informed of the sinking of the *Lusitania*.

ANSWERS

1. Roberto DeVincenzo, who lost to Bob Goalby

2. Jacqueline Pung will always be thanked by the winner, Betsy Rawls.

3. Gene Littler entered 26 Masters between 1954 and 1980, winning none.

4. Heard finished his round and ended up in fourth place for the tournament.

5. Tommy Armour, at the Shawnee Inn Golf Club

6. Wayne Grady

7. Greg Norman and Craig Wood

8. Seve Ballesteros

9. Tom Kite was captured on tape at the 1991 Byron Nelson Classic.

10. Woodrow Wilson, who returned immediately to the White House

CHIP SHOTS

"Ninety percent of the putts that fall short don't go in."

–Yogi Berra

WHO SAID IT ...

1. "Most people retire to play golf and fish. I do that now." Lee Trevino or Julius Boros?

2. "I did my best, but chasing Nicklaus is like chasing a walking record book." Tom Weiskopf or Tom Watson?

3. "My goal is to become filthy rich. But obviously, that isn't going to be in golf." Johnny Miller or Gary McCord?

4. "If a great swing put you high on the money list, there'd be some of us who would be broke." Raymond Floyd or Nick Faldo?

5. "Anytime a golfer hits a ball perfectly straight with a big club, it is, in my view, a fluke." Walter Hagen or Jack Nicklaus?

6. "When I was younger, I was 'an angry player'. Now all of a sudden I'm a 'fiery competitor'. I like the change in vocabulary." Corey Pavin or Greg Norman?

7. "Bad sausage and five bogeys will give you a stomach ache every time." Miller Barber or Craig Stadler?

8. "The reason the Road Hole at St. Andrews is the most difficult par-4 in the world is that it was designed as a par-6." Ian Woosnam or Ben Crenshaw?

9. "If this was any tournament but The Masters, I'd have shot 66. But I was choking out there. That green coat plays castanets with your knees." Chi Chi Rodriguez or Jose Maria Olazabal?

10. "The difference between me and an amateur is that I'm not afraid to screw up." John Daly or Fuzzy Zoeller?

ANSWERS

1. Julius Boros
2. Top Weiskopf
3. Gary McCord
4. Raymond Floyd
5. Jack Nicklaus
6. Corey Pavin
7. Miller Barber
8. Ben Crenshaw
9. Chi Chi Rodriguez
10. Fuzzy Zoeller

CHIP SHOTS

"I know I'm getting better at golf because I'm hitting fewer spectators."

–*President Gerald R. Ford*

TRUE OR FALSE?

1. The PGA Championship was once decided by match play.

2. Charley Seaver, a member of the 1932 U.S. Walker Cup team, is the father of Tom Seaver, baseball Hall of Fame pitcher.

3. Former Colorado defensive back Hale Irwin played one year of pro football before joining the PGA Tour.

4. Lee Trevino is one of a long line of golfers who attended the University of Texas.

5. Nathanial Crosby, son of singer Bing Crosby, once won the U.S. Amateur.

6. Yale University has won the most NCAA Team Golf Championships.

7. Senior PGA Tour golfer Jay Sigel never played on the regular Tour, but did win two U.S. Amateur titles.

8. Byron Nelson won the 1943 U.S. Open.

9. Gary Player never won the PGA's Player of the Year award in his career.

10. Kathy Whitworth, the career leader in wins on any tour with 88, never won the U.S. Women's Open.

ANSWERS

1. True — The 1958 championship was the first decided by stroke play.

2. True

3. False

4. False — Trevino never attended college.

5. True — Crosby was the top male amateur in 1981.

6. True — Yale has won it 21 times.

7. True — He was top amateur in 1982 and '83.

8. False — The Open that year was canceled because of World War II.

9. True

10. True — Whitworth won six majors in her career, but the Open wasn't one of them.

Chip Shots

"I was three over — one over a house, one over a patio and one over a swimming pool."

–George Brett, Hall of Fame pro baseball player but amateur golfer

AMATEUR NIGHT

1. I'm the last amateur golfer to win a U.S. Open title, capturing it in 1933. Who am I?

2. This 18-year-old shot a final-round 69 to win the 2000 Australian Open, becoming the first amateur since 1960 to take the title. Name him.

3. Who was the first amateur to win the U.S. Women's Open?

4. These two University of Texas teammates finished tied for the individual collegiate championship in 1972. Who are they?

5. In 1981, the U.S. Post Office came out with a stamp honoring this male Hall of Fame golfer. Who was he?

6. If a Walker Cup match is tied, which team (United States or Great Britain and Ireland) keeps the cup?

7. Who was the first golfer to repeat as U.S. Junior Amateur champion?

8. What golfer won the U.S. Amateur in 1974 and, two years later, was the U.S. Open champion?

9. Three native Texans have won the U.S. Amateur. Billy Maxwell and Scott Verplank are two of them. Who's the third?

10. Who was the first amateur to win the U.S. Open?

ANSWERS

1. Johnny Goodman

2. Aaron Baddeley

3. Catherine Lacoste of France, in 1967

4. Ben Crenshaw and Tom Kite

5. Bobby Jones

6. In the event of a tie, the Cup is retained for another two years by the previous winner.

7. Eldrick "Tiger" Woods won the event in 1991, '92 and '93.

8. Jerry Pate

9. Justin Leonard

10. Francis Ouimet won the Open in 1913.

Chip Shots

"How did I four-putt? I missed the hole.
I missed the hole. I missed the hole. I made it."

–Fuzzy Zoeller

LEGAL OR ILLEGAL?

You decide if the situations listed below are within the rules of golf.

1. Just before putting, I use my club to flatten a few spike marks which are on my line.

2. I ask you what club you just hit.

3. With my ball in a bunker, I touch the sand with my club to determine its condition.

4. After being struck, my ball accidentally hits my golf cart.

5. I swing at my ball and top it. When it's in the air, my club strikes it a second time.

6. My ball is in the fairway and a loose twig is touching it. I pick up the twig and, in the process, my ball moves.

7. My ball is overhanging the lip of the cup and I wait two minutes. At that point, the ball falls into the cup.

8. During a match, you putt your ball and it hits my caddie.

9. A live bug is crawling on your ball on the green. You mark your ball, pick it up, blow the bug off and replace the ball.

10. My driver breaks after hitting a ball during a match and I replace it.

ANSWERS

1. Illegal — As a result, I am assessed a two-stroke penalty.

2. Illegal — It's a two-stroke penalty for me, but if you answer me, you also get a two-stroke penalty.

3. Illegal — I am assessed a two-stroke penalty.

4. Illegal — It's a two-stroke penalty and I play the ball where it lies.

5. Illegal, with a one-stroke penalty — If I was lying three before the first swing, I now lie five.

6. Illegal — I am assessed a one-stroke penalty.

7. Illegal — I am assessed a one-stroke penalty. If it was my fourth shot, I get a five for the hole.

8. There is no penalty. You may accept the stroke and let the ball lie where it is, or cancel the stroke, return the ball to its original position, and retake the shot.

9. There is no penalty.

10. Legal, if I don't delay play — However, if I've broken it in a fit of anger, I can't replace it.

LINGO OF THE LINKS

1. What's the modern-day name for the *niblick*?

2. What is an *albatross*?

3. What's the modern-day name for the *mashie*?

4. What's the difference between match play and medal play?

5. What does the phrase *through the green* mean?

6. You're my caddie as I play the back nine of the British Open. I ask for my *jigger*. What club do you hand me?

7. What's a *stymie*?

8. What's the term for a slice that starts left and then fades?

9. What's a *featherie*?

10. What's a *muni*?

CHIP SHOTS

"The way I putted, I must have been reading the greens in Spanish and putting them in English."

–Homero Blancas

ANSWERS

1. The 9-iron

2. It's the British term for a double-eagle.

3. The 5-iron

4. The winner at match play is determined by the total holes won, while medal play is by total strokes.

5. It means the entire golf course except the teeing ground, the putting green and all hazards. Out-of-bounds is, of course, not considered to be part of the course.

6. The 4-iron

7. An intentional putt between an opponent's ball and the hole without marking the ball — Thus, the opponent is forced to putt around the ball. The stymie is an illegal shot.

8. You've just hit a *banana ball*.

9. A golf ball used until about 1850, the featherie was a leather sack filled with wet goose feathers. As the feathers dried, they expanded and made the ball hard.

10. A municipal golf course

CHIP SHOTS

"I'll take a two-shot penalty, but I'll be damned if I'm going to play the ball where it lies."

-Elaine Johnson, after her shot hit a tree and caromed into her bra

GOLF GEOGRAPHY

1. Where was the first Ryder Cup played in 1927?

2. This NJ course is continually ranked as one of the best in the world. Although two Walker Cup matches have been held there, the course has never hosted a U.S. Open. Name it.

3. Excluding the British Isles, what country had the first golf course?

4. Where is the Oakland Hills Country Club, site of numerous major championships, located?

5. The Inverness Club was the site of two playoff losses by Greg Norman in the PGA Championship. Where's it located?

6. This famous seaside course with its 107-yard, par-3 7th hole was designed by amateur golfer Jack Neville in 1919. Name it.

7. Name the native country of Vijay Singh.

8. Name the Scottish course where the first twelve British Opens were contested.

9. Not counting Antarctica, which continent has the least golfers and the fewest golf courses in the world?

10. Name the golf club that hosted the first U.S. Open in 1895.

ANSWERS

1. The Worcester Country Club in Massachusetts
2. Pine Valley Golf Club in Clementon, NJ
3. India — The Royal Calcutta Golf Club was established in 1829.
4. Birmingham, Michigan
5. Toledo, Ohio
6. Pebble Beach Golf Links in California
7. Fiji
8. Prestwick Golf Club
9. South America
10. The Newport (RI) Golf Club

Chip Shots

"Heck, I wish they'd make the gallery ropes out of bounds. We're the only sport that plays in the audience."

–Lee Trevino

THE MASTERS

1. What was the original name of the tournament?

2. Who was the youngest golfer to win The Masters — Jack Nicklaus or Seve Ballesteros?

3. Nicklaus was the first player to win back-to-back titles. Who was the second?

4. True or false? The Masters was the first major to switch from an 18-hole playoff to sudden death.

5. In 1978, he trailed Hubert Green by seven strokes going into the final day, but a record-tying 64 put him into the third green jacket of his career. Who was he?

6. Name the first golfer to win The Masters four times.

7. What American president was a member of the Augusta National Golf Club?

8. Who was the first player to win The Masters in his initial appearance at Augusta?

9. True or false? Broadcasters at The Masters refer to the paying customers as the *gallery*.

10. Who was the winner of the first Masters tournament in 1934?

ANSWERS

1. The Augusta National Invitation Tournament
2. Ballesteros was three months younger than Nicklaus was when he won his first championship.
3. Nick Faldo won in 1989 and '90.
4. True
5. Gary Player
6. Arnold Palmer
7. Dwight D. Eisenhower
8. Fuzzy Zoeller won it in 1979.
9. False — They are called *patrons*.
10. Horton Smith

Chip Shots

"I went to bed and I was old and washed up. I woke up a rookie. What could be better?"

–Raymond Floyd, after becoming the big 5-0 and qualifying for the Senior Tour

FOUR-LETTER PROS

The answers in this quiz all have four-letter last names.
Do you know ...

1. The winner of the first British Open?

2. The ninth alternate who came out of nowhere to win the
   1991 PGA Championship?

3. The golfer who shot a record-tying 59 at the 1991
   Las Vegas Invitational?

4. The 1959 Masters champ who came back from six strokes
   down to win?

5. The North Carolina golfer who taught fellow Tarheel,
   Michael Jordan, the game of golf?

6. The 1985 British Open and 1988 Masters champion?

7. The player who lost the 1939 U.S. Open in a playoff, only to
   come back and win the title two years later?

8. The Hall of Famer who has won the most major
   championships on the LPGA Tour?

9. The man who chipped in from 35 yards out on the second
   hole of sudden death to win the 1987 Masters?

10. The golfer whose first major win came at the age of 42 at
    the 1992 U.S. Open?

ANSWERS

1. Willie Park
2. John Daly
3. Chip Beck
4. Art Wall
5. Davis Love III
6. Sandy Lyle
7. Craig Wood
8. Patty Berg
9. Larry Mize
10. Tom Kite

CHIP SHOTS

"Golf is twenty percent mechanics and technique. The other eighty percent is philosophy, humor, tragedy, romance, melodrama, companionship, camaraderie, cussedness and conversation."

–Grantland Rice

SCHOOL DAYS

Match the golfer with the school attended.

1. John Cook
2. Justin Leonard
3. Tom Lehman
4. Hale Irwin
5. Fred Couples
6. Raymond Floyd
7. Phil Mickelson
8. Corey Pavin
9. John Daly
10. Tom Watson

A) Arizona State
B) Houston
C) UCLA
D) Ohio State
E) Arkansas
F) Colorado
G) Minnesota
H) Stanford
I) Texas
J) North Carolina

CHIP SHOTS

"Never bet with anyone you meet on the first tee who has a deep suntan, a one-iron in his bag and squinty eyes."

–Dave Marr

ANSWERS

1. D
2. I
3. G
4. F
5. B
6. J
7. A
8. C
9. E
10. H

Chip Shots

"I owe a lot to my parents, especially
my mother and father."

-*Greg Norman*

THE GOLDEN BEAR

How much do you know about Jack Nicklaus?

1. What age was Nicklaus when he became the oldest Masters champion in 1986?

2. His twenty major victories are seven more than his closest competitor. Who is he?

3. True or false? Nicklaus was the first player to win the Pebble Beach National Pro-Am and the U.S. Open in the same year.

4. How many British Opens did he win?

5. His first try at the Senior Tour resulted in a win at what tournament in 1990?

6. What Pennsylvania course was the site of his first victory as a pro, the 1962 U.S. Open?

7. What golfer did Nicklaus beat in a playoff for the title?

8. The Open was his first win as a pro. At what tournament did he make his pro debut?

9. How many consecutive years did Nicklaus win at least one PGA Tour event?
   a) 11   b) 13   c) 15   d) 17

10. How many times in his career did the Golden Bear win at least two of the four Grand Slam events in the same year?

ANSWERS

1. He was 46 years old.

2. Bobby Jones

3. True — The 1972 U.S. Open was held at Pebble Beach.

4. Three — in 1966, '70 and '78

5. The Tradition

6. Oakmont CC

7. Arnold Palmer

8. Nicklaus debuted at the 1962 Los Angeles Open, earning $33.33.

9. Seventeen, from 1962-78

10. He did it five times, in 1963, '66, '72, '75 and '80.

Chip shots

"I wish my name was Tom Kite."

-Ian Baker-Finch, on signing autographs

HEADLINE/DATELINE

Match the news with the date on which it occurred.

1. WHITWORTH WINS
   4TH LPGA TITLE

2. SNEAD BEATS HOGAN
   FOR MASTERS

3. HOGAN HURT IN CRASH

4. NICKLAUS WINS 5TH PGA

5. WOODS, 18,
   WINS U.S. AMATEUR

6. MILLER CAPTURES
   U.S. OPEN

7. SHEPARD PLAYS
   6-IRON ON MOON

8. PALMER WINS MASTERS,
   HIS 1ST MAJOR

9. HAGEN WINS
   4TH STRAIGHT PGA

10. GEIBERGER FIRST
    TO FIRE 59

A) June 10, 1977

B) November 5, 1927

C) February 2, 1949

D) February 5, 1971

E) April 6, 1958

F) June 1, 1975

G) June 17, 1973

H) August 28, 1994

I) August 10, 1980

J) April 12, 1954

ANSWERS

1. F
2. J
3. C
4. I
5. H
6. G
7. D
8. E
9. B
10. A

CHIP SHOTS

"If you can't break 80, you have no business playing golf. If you can break 80, you have no business."

–British adage

PUTTER POTPOURRI

1. The PGA Tour record for winning the same event the most times is eight. Who did it?

2. Besides the golf, what was unique about the 1922 U.S. Open?

3. What LPGA player receives the Vare Trophy at the end of the year?

4. True or false? Golfers have to be 50 years old to play in the U.S. Senior Open, but 55 years old to enter the U.S. Senior Amateur.

5. I played in 113 consecutive events on the PGA Tour without missing a cut, a record. Who am I?

6. Name the winner of the 2000 Masters.

7. Of all the players to ever win a major title, who comes first alphabetically?

8. In the nineteenth century, most golf shafts were made of what type of wood?

9. Quick! Which state has the most golf courses?

10. Who was the first African-American to play in The Masters?

ANSWERS

1. Sam Snead won the Greater Greensboro Open eight times.

2. It was the first time admission was charged for the Open. The price of a ticket was one dollar.

3. It's awarded to the player with the lowest scoring average for the year.

4. True

5. Byron Nelson

6. Vijay Singh

7. Tommy Aaron, who won the 1973 Masters

8. Hickory

9. Florida, with California a close second

10. Lee Elder, who competed in the 1975 tournament

CHIP SHOTS

"Cypress Point is so exclusive that it had a membership drive and drove out forty members."

–Bob Hope

SCRAMBLE

The following golfers won one major title in their careers.
Unscramble the names for the answers.

1. NAYEW DRAGY
2. ANI KRABE CFNIH
3. TCOTS POMSSIN
4. GIRAC TLADERS
5. YOREC VIPAN
6. AULP WIERAL
7. OMT TEIK
8. RACHSEL YODOC
9. LIVLERO DOOMY
10. KARM LACVACHICECA

Chip Shots

"Some hotel rugs are impossible to putt."

–Tom Watson

ANSWERS

1. Wayne Grady — 1990 PGA Championship
2. Ian Baker-Finch — 1991 British Open
3. Scott Simpson — 1987 U.S. Open
4. Craig Stadler — 1982 Masters
5. Corey Pavin — 1995 U.S. Open
6. Paul Lawrie — 1999 British Open
7. Tom Kite — 1992 U.S. Open
8. Charles Coody — 1971 Masters
9. Orville Moody — 1969 U.S. Open
10. Mark Calcavecchia — 1989 British Open

Chip Shots

"The toughest hole is the nineteenth. I just can't get through it. It takes the longest time to play."

–Craig Stadler

THE UNSTOPPABLES

Name the golfers who put together these hot streaks.

1. He set the record in 1945 with eleven straight PGA Tour wins.

2. He retired from competitive golf after winning the four majors in 1930.

3. After his disappointing finishes in the 1986 majors, he spent the autumn winning five straight tournaments — two in Europe and three in Australia.

4. He started the 1974 season winning the first three PGA Tour events, finishing with eight wins in all, a year after his U.S. Open triumph.

5. This LPGA Hall of Famer racked up thirteen wins in 1963, including four straight, her best season ever.

6. This rookie set the LPGA record when she won five straight tour events in 1978.

7. Enter three majors, win three majors. 1953 was a very good year for this man.

8. He captured the U.S., Canadian and British Opens in a four-week span in 1971.

9. Before she turned pro, this founding member of the LPGA won seventeen straight amateur events in 1946-47.

10. Five years before winning The Masters, this 20-year-old won eight events in his debut on the PGA Tour.

ANSWERS

1. Byron Nelson
2. Bobby Jones
3. Greg Norman
4. Johnny Miller
5. Mickey Wright
6. Nancy Lopez
7. Ben Hogan
8. Lee Trevino
9. Babe Zaharias
10. Horton Smith

CHIP SHOTS

"Another weekend with nothing to do."

–Arnold Palmer, after missing a cut

DUFFER'S DILEMMA

You decide which of the golfers is the correct answer.

1. He was voted the best golfer in history in a poll in *Golf Digest*. Was it Bobby Jones or Jack Nicklaus?

2. He was the first golfer from Great Britain to win The Masters. Was it Nick Faldo or Sandy Lyle?

3. He was the second golfer in history to win $1 million in his career. Was it Billy Casper or Raymond Floyd?

4. He had 17 wins on the PGA Tour before reaching his 30th birthday. Was it Lee Trevino or Johnny Miller?

5. He was the first golfer to win PGA Tour titles in four different decades. Was it Sam Snead or Arnold Palmer?

6. He led the PGA Tour in driving accuracy ten straight years, 1981-90. Was it Gary Player or Calvin Peete?

7. He was the first South African golfer to win the British Open. Was it Ernie Els or Bobby Locke?

8. She won the most major championships in LPGA Tour history. Was it Patty Berg or Pat Bradley?

9. He was the first golfer to use a female caddie while playing in The Masters. Was it George Archer or Nick Faldo?

10. She's second on the list, behind Kathy Whitworth, of golfers with the most LPGA tournament wins. Is it Laura Davies or Mickey Wright?

ANSWERS

1. Jack Nicklaus

2. Sandy Lyle, 1988

3. Billy Casper

4. Johnny Miller

5. Sam Snead

6. Calvin Peete

7. Bobby Locke first won in 1949. He also won it in 1950, '52 and '57.

8. Patty Berg won 16 majors in her career.

9. George Archer's daughter caddied for him in the 1983 tournament.

10. Mickey Wright won 82 tournaments in her career.

CHIP SHOTS

"Columbus went around the world in 1492. That isn't a lot of strokes when you consider the course."

–Lee Trevino

GIVE ME A VOWEL

Here's a list of two-time U.S. Open winners with the vowels
removed from their first and last names.
The order of the consonants has not been changed.
The years they won the title may help you out.

1. GNSRZN, 1922 and '32
2. LXSMTH, 1906 and '10
3. JLSBRS, 1952 and '63
4. BLLYCSPR, 1959 and '66
5. LTRVN, 1968 and '71
6. NDYNRTH, 1978 and '85
7. RNLS, 1994 and '97
8. PYNSTWRT, 1991 and '99
9. CRTSSTRNG, 1988 and '89
10. LJNZN, 1993 and '98

Chip Shots

"I'm the best. I just haven't played yet."

–Muhammad Ali, on golf

ANSWERS

1. Gene Sarazen
2. Alex Smith
3. Julius Boros
4. Billy Casper
5. Lee Trevino
6. Andy North
7. Ernie Els
8. Payne Stewart
9. Curtis Strange
10. Lee Janzen

Chip shots

"Golfers find it a very trying matter to turn at the waist, more particularly if they have a lot of waist to turn."

–Harry Vardon

THE BRITISH OPEN

1. Who was the winner of the first British Open?

2. Who was the first American to win the title?

3. This father-son duo won eight of the first twelve Opens. Who were they?

4. Only three golfers have won the Open in three different decades. Harry Vardon and J.H. Taylor are two of them. Who's the third?

5. Who is the only golfer to win six British Opens?

6. True or false? It wasn't until 1948 that a British monarch attended the Open.

7. 1963 was the only year that a left-handed golfer won the tournament. Who was that southpaw?

8. When was the Open first televised?

9. Name the Scottish golfer who won at Carnoustie in a playoff against Jean Van de Velde and Justin Leonard.

10. 1966 was the first year the British Open was played over four days. What American came home with the title?

ANSWERS

1. Willie Park, 1860

2. Walter Hagen, who first won the tournament in 1922

3. Tom Morris, Sr. and Jr. — They are also known as Old Tom Morris and Young Tom Morris.

4. Gary Player

5. Harry Vardon, who won it in 1896, '98, '99, 1903, '11 and '14

6. True — The monarch was King George VI.

7. Bob Charles of New Zealand

8. 1955

9. Paul Lawrie, in 1999

10. Jack Nicklaus

CHIP SHOTS

"If I had it my way, any man guilty of golf would be ineligible for any office of trust in the United States."

–H.L. Mencken

BY THE NUMBERS

Do you know ...

1. The number of clubs allowed in tournament competition?

2. Within ten yards, the distance a golf ball with no dimples will fly?

3. The odds against an amateur golfer recording a single hole-in-one?

4. The depth of a golf hole?

5. The average score for 18 holes for the average golfer, according to the National Golf Foundation?

6. The number of dimples, to the nearest hundred, on the modern golf ball?

7. The diameter of a golf ball?

8. The diameter of a golf hole?

9. The most common 18-hole par on golf courses around the world?

10. The number of founders of the LPGA?

ANSWERS

1. Fourteen

2. Sixty to eighty yards before dropping quickly back to earth

3. Approximately 43,000 to one

4. Four inches

5. 97 — Only one-third of all golfers regularly break 90.

6. 400

7. 1.68 inches

8. 4.25 inches

9. 72

10. Four — Patty Berg, Betty Jameson, Louise Suggs and Babe Zaharias

CHIP SHOTS

"You all know Jerry Ford — the most dangerous driver since Ben Hur."

–Bob Hope

OPEN SEASON

Match the U.S. Open winner with the course where he triumphed.

1. Tom Watson, 1982
2. Jack Nicklaus, 1980
3. Corey Pavin, 1995
4. Hale Irwin, 1990
5. Fuzzy Zoeller, 1984
6. Ken Venturi, 1964
7. Ben Hogan, 1953
8. Curtis Strange, 1988
9. Arnold Palmer, 1960
10. Lee Trevino, 1971

A) Shinnecock Hills GC
B) Winged Foot GC
C) The Country Club
D) Cherry Hills CC
E) Congressional CC
F) Merion GC
G) Baltusrol GC
H) Pebble Beach Golf Links
I) Medinah CC
J) Oakmont CC

Chip Shots

"Tiger Woods? I thought that was a golf course."

–Sandy Lyle, on then-amateur golfer Tiger Woods

ANSWERS

1. H
2. G
3. A
4. I
5. B
6. E
7. J
8. C
9. D
10. F

Chip Shots

"Swing hard in case you hit it."

–Dan Marino

LADIES' CHOICE

Test your knowledge of the Ladies Professional Golf Association.

1. What year was the LPGA formed?

2. In 1983, she became the youngest player on the Tour to earn more than $1 million in her career. Who was she?

3. Name the two Hall of Famers who combined for 170 career victories on the Tour.

4. What was Babe Zaharias' real name?

5. Who was the first foreigner to pass the million dollar mark in her career?

6. When was the first LPGA Tour event televised?

7. What golfer won the Vare Trophy, for lowest scoring average, a record seven times in her career?

8. In 1969, I won the U.S. Women's Amateur, two years after walking away with the U.S. Women's Open title. Who am I?

9. Her hole-in-one in the 1959 U.S. Women's Open made her the first woman to record an ace in USGA competition. Name her.

10. Who was the first golfer to win all four LPGA majors in her career?

ANSWERS

1. 1950

2. Nancy Lopez — She broke the barrier in 1983.

3. Kathy Whitworth and Mickey Wright — The two also finished second 140 times between them.

4. Mildred Ella Zaharias — She got the nickname, Babe, when she hit five home runs in a baseball game as a kid.

5. Australian Jan Stephenson

6. 1963 — ABC carried the final round of the U.S. Women's Open.

7. Kathy Whitworth

8. Catherine Lacoste

9. Patty Berg

10. Pat Bradley

CHIP SHOTS

"Have you ever noticed what golf spells backwards?"

–Al Boliska

FAVORITE SONS

Each of the following winners of a major has a last name ending in *son*. How many can you get?

1. Winner of the U.S. Open in 1983 and the PGA Championship in 1981 and '87

2. Winner of five British Opens

3. The only LPGA major she didn't win was the Dinah Shore.

4. The only PGA major he didn't win was the British Open.

5. This Australian won five British Opens (in 1954, '55, '56, '58 and '65).

6. The first dominating player in America in the 20th century, he won four U.S. Opens, including three in a row.

7. His only major triumph came in the 1987 U.S. Open at The Olympic Club.

8. 1992 LPGA Rookie of the Year, whose first victory came at the 1993 Dinah Shore

9. His bid for four straight titles ended in 1884, losing in the first playoff in British Open history.

10. A founding mother of the LPGA, her win came at the 1947 U.S. Women's Open.

ANSWERS

1. Larry Nelson
2. Tom Watson
3. Jan Stephenson
4. Byron Nelson
5. Peter Thomson
6. Willie Anderson
7. Scott Simpson
8. Helen Alfredsson
9. Bob Ferguson
10. Betty Jameson

CHIP SHOTS

"When I told the career guidance person I wanted to be a golf professional, he said that there's no such thing as a golf professional."

–Bernhard Langer

TRUE OR FALSE?

1. Golf was once an Olympic sport.

2. Bob Charles is the only lefty to finish a U.S. Open at par or better.

3. Nick Faldo is the only player to win two Masters playoffs.

4. Before the invention of the wooden tee, sand was used to raise the ball.

5. Tom Watson and Jack Nicklaus attended the same college.

6. Ben Hogan was born in Dublin, Ireland.

7. Pat Bradley won every major on the LPGA Tour at least once in her career.

8. The British Amateur Championship began before the British Open.

9. More golf is shown at The Masters than any other televised event.

10. Chi Chi Rodriguez never won a major in his PGA career.

ANSWERS

1. True — It was played in the 1900 and 1904 Olympics.

2. False — Phil Mickelson has done it.

3. True

4. True

5. False — Watson went to Stanford, while Nicklaus attended Ohio State.

6. False — Hogan was born in Dublin, *Texas*.

7. True

8. False — The Amateur began in 1885, 25 years after the first professional Open.

9. True — Only four minutes of commercials per hour are allowed by Masters' officials.

10. True

Chip Shots

> "Tranquilizers make it possible for a golfer to relax at his favorite form of relaxation."
>
> *–Writer Stephen Baker*

THREE ON A MATCH

1. Name one of the three golfers who have U.S. Postal stamps honoring them.

2. Who are the only two U.S. Open winners with exactly three letters in their last names?

3. What three majors has Lee Trevino won in his career?

4. Only one man has won the U.S. Open in three different decades. Name him.

5. Since 1950, three players with exactly four letters in their last names have won the British Open. Who are they?

6. Name the only three golfers to compete in over 30 consecutive U.S. Opens.

7. Three golfers who defeated Greg Norman in major championship playoffs have the letter "z" in their last names. How many do you know?

8. Name three golfers who entered the LPGA Hall of Fame in the 1990s.

9. Who are the only three players to win the British Open in three different decades?

10. An amateur has finished second at The Masters three times, the last being Charlie Coe in 1961. Do you know the other two golfers?

ANSWERS

1. Bobby Jones, Babe Zaharias and Francis Ouimet

2. Edward "Ted" Ray, 1920 and Ernie Els, 1994 and '97

3. The U.S. Open, 1968 and '71; British Open, 1971 and '72; and the PGA Championship, 1974

4. Jack Nicklaus in the '60s, '70s and '80s

5. Tony Lema, 1964; Sandy Lyle, 1985; and John Daly, 1995

6. Gene Sarazen, Arnold Palmer and Jack Nicklaus

7. Fuzzy Zoeller won the 1984 U.S. Open; Larry Mize captured the 1987 Masters; and, Paul Azinger won at the 1993 PGA Championship.

8. Pat Bradley, 1991; Patsy Sheehan, 1993; Betsy King, 1995; and Juli Inkster, 1999

9. Harry Vardon, J.H. Taylor and Gary Player

10. Frank Stranahan, 1947 and Ken Venturi, 1956

CHIP SHOTS

"Baseball players quit playing and they take up golf. Basketball players quit, take up golf. Football players quit, take up golf. What are we supposed to take up when we quit?"

–George Archer

THE HAWK

How much do you know about Ben Hogan?

1. What is Hogan's real first name?

2. Name the course dubbed "Hogan's Alley" because of his numerous victories there, including the 1948 U.S. Open.

3. True or false? Hogan's 1953 British Open win came in his first, and only, attempt for the title.

4. At what Scottish course did he triumph?

5. 1953 was the year Hogan won five of the six tournaments he entered. What was the only one he lost?

6. That year he won all the majors except the PGA Championship. Why did Hogan have no chance to win the PGA?

7. Glenn Ford had the title role in a movie about Ben Hogan. What was the name of the movie?

8. Hogan's bid for a fifth U.S. Open title ended in a playoff with this PGA Tour unknown in 1955. Who was it?

9. What was the irony of the upstart's victory?

10. How many times did Hogan win The Masters?

ANSWERS

1. He was born William Benjamin Hogan.

2. The Riviera Country Club in Los Angeles, CA

3. True

4. Carnoustie

5. The Greenbrier Open in White Sulphur Springs, West Virginia — Sam Snead was the winner.

6. It was held the same week as the British Open.

7. *Follow the Sun*

8. Jack Fleck

9. Fleck won the Open with a set of Ben Hogan golf clubs.

10. Hogan won two Masters, in 1951 and '53.

CHIP SHOTS

"Be funny on a golf course? Do I kid my best friend's mother about her heart condition?"

–Comedian Phil Silvers

SECONDHAND CLUBS

Match the golfers who won these major championship
playoffs with the players who finished second.

1. Gene Sarazen, 1935 Masters

2. Byron Nelson, 1943 U.S. Open

3. Jack Nicklaus, 1962 U.S. Open

4. Lee Trevino, 1971 U.S. Open

5. Tom Watson, 1975 British Open

6. Paul Azinger, 1993
   PGA Championship

7. Curtis Strange, 1988 U.S. Open

8. Nick Faldo, 1990 Masters

9. David Graham, 1979
   PGA Championship

10. Payne Stewart, 1991 U.S. Open

A) Nick Faldo

B) Jack Newton

C) Scott Simpson

D) Ben Hogan

E) Raymond Floyd

F) Craig Wood

G) Ben Crenshaw

H) Arnold Palmer

I) Greg Norman

J) Jack Nicklaus

ANSWERS

1. F
2. D
3. H
4. J
5. B
6. I
7. A
8. E
9. G
10. C

Chip Shots

"What is love compared with holing out before your opponent?"

–P.G. Wodehouse

MORE FRIED EGGS AND UNPLAYABLE LIES

1. In the 1983 British Open, this golfer missed a three-inch putt when he tried to tap the ball with a backhand stroke. He lost the championship by one stroke. Who was he?

2. His attempt to become the first amateur to win The Masters went up in smoke when he shot a closing 80 to lose the 1956 tournament by one. Name him.

3. A quadruple bogey on the fifth hole of the final round, including a penalty for a double hit, cost him a four-stroke lead at the 1985 U.S. Open. He lost by one stroke. Who was he?

4. Whose double bogey on the final hole of the 1961 Masters turned a one-stroke win into a one-stroke loss for him?

5. Name the golfer who lost a nine-stroke lead over the final twenty-seven holes of the 1990 U.S. Woman's Open.

6. Who missed a two-foot putt for victory on the first playoff hole at the 1989 Masters?

7. All he had to do was sink a three-foot putt to win the 1970 British Open. His miss put him into a playoff against Jack Nicklaus, which he lost. Who was he?

8. Who shot a 78 at the 1996 Masters to become the only golfer to lose a six-stroke 54-hole lead in a major?

9. Needing just a double bogey on the final hole to become the 1999 British Open champion, he made a triple. Name him.

10. In 1993, Greg Norman became the first British Open champion to break seventy in all four rounds of the tournament. But he wasn't the first golfer to do it. Name the player who did it first, but still finished tied for sixth.

ANSWERS

1. Hale Irwin
2. Ken Venturi
3. T.C. Chen
4. Arnold Palmer
5. Patty Sheehan
6. Scott Hoch
7. Doug Sanders
8. Greg Norman
9. Jean Van de Velde
10. Ernie Els

Chip Shots

"My putter will not be flying first class home with me."

–Nick Faldo

THE U.S. OPEN

1. In 1968, he became the first golfer to play four sub-70 rounds at a U.S. Open. Who was he?

2. What Open championship was the first to be televised nationally?

3. Who was the first Australian to win an Open?

4. Name the state where Shinnecock Hills GC, host to three U.S. Opens, is located.

5. Two golfers beat Arnold Palmer in Open playoffs in consecutive years in the '60s. One was Jack Nicklaus. Who was the other player?

6. Name the golf club that hosted the first U.S. Open in 1895.

7. I'm the first player to win the U.S. Junior Amateur, U.S. Amateur and U.S. Open. Who am I?

8. He posted the lowest score ever shot by an amateur at the 1960 U.S. Open, shooting a 282. Who was he?

9. What Open was the first to be held at a facility open to the public?

10. Name the two golfers who participated in the first sudden-death playoff to decide the Open.

ANSWERS

1. Lee Trevino
2. The 1954 Open at Baltusrol GC, won by Ed Furgol
3. David Graham
4. New York
5. 1963 Open winner Julius Boros
6. The Newport (RI) Golf Club
7. Tiger Woods
8. Jack Nicklaus
9. The 1972 Open, which was held at Pebble Beach Golf Links
10. Hale Irwin made an 8-foot birdie putt on the 91st hole to beat Mike Donald in 1990.

CHIP SHOTS

"I love to watch *Oprah, Geraldo*, all the shows about dysfunctionals. That's my psychoanalysis. I realized I wasn't as bad as I thought."

–*Golfer Mac O'Grady*

HEADLINE/DATELINE

Match the news with the date on which it occurred.

1. BRADLEY INDUCTED INTO LPGA HALL

2. NICKLAUS CAPTURES 2ND PGA TITLE

3. SMITH WINS INAUGURAL MASTERS

4. FIRST RYDER CUP TO USA

5. HOGAN TAKES RECORD 4TH U.S. OPEN

6. FIRST MAJOR WIN FOR ELS

7. TRIO STRUCK BY LIGHTNING AT WESTERN

8. LORD BYRON WINS 11TH STRAIGHT

9. LONGSHOT DALY PGA CHAMP

10. JONES COMPLETES GRAND SLAM

A) August 4, 1945

B) March 25, 1934

C) June 27, 1975

D) February 28, 1971

E) August 11, 1991

F) June 4, 1927

G) September 27, 1930

H) January 18, 1992

I) June 20, 1994

J) June 13, 1953

ANSWERS

1. H
2. D
3. B
4. F
5. J
6. I
7. C
8. A
9. E
10. G

CHIP SHOTS

"The devoted golfer is an anguished soul who has learned a lot about putting just as an avalanche victim has learned a lot about snow."

–Writer Dan Jenkins

SCRAMBLE

Listed below are U.S. Amateur champions who
went on to successful careers on the PGA Tour.
Unscramble their names for the answers.

1. GREIT ODOSW
2. STUIJN NRLEADO
3. HLIP KLESICONM
4. TCSOT PNKALRVE
5. ALH TSOTUN
6. RMKA OAREMA
7. HONJ OCKO
8. IRCAG DARLEST
9. NAYNL KDINWSA
10. CJKA LCAKUNIS

Chip Shots

"If you call on God to improve the results of a
shot while it is still in motion, you are using
'an outside agency' and are subject to appropriate
penalties under the rules of golf."

–Henry Longhurst

ANSWERS

1. Tiger Woods
2. Justin Leonard
3. Phil Mickelson
4. Scott Verplank
5. Hal Sutton
6. Mark O'Meara
7. John Cook
8. Craig Stadler
9. Lanny Wadkins
10. Jack Nicklaus

Chip Shots

"The difference between golf and government is that in golf you can't improve your lie."

–George Deukmejian

SCHOOL DAYS II

Match the golfer with the college he attended.

1. Paul Azinger
2. Tiger Woods
3. Chip Beck
4. Ben Crenshaw
5. Lee Janzen
6. Davis Love III
7. David Duval
8. Payne Stewart
9. Curtis Strange
10. Fuzzy Zoeller

A) Southern Methodist University
B) Florida Southern
C) North Carolina
D) Stanford
E) Houston
F) Florida State
G) Wake Forest
H) Georgia
I) Georgia Tech
J) Texas

CHIP SHOTS

"Anything I want it to be. For instance, the hole right here is a par-47, and yesterday I birdied the sucker."

– Country singer Willie Nelson, on being asked what was par on a Texas golf course he owns

ANSWERS

1. F
2. D
3. H
4. J
5. B
6. C
7. I
8. A
9. G
10. E

CHIP SHOTS

"My swing is so bad I look like a caveman killing his lunch."

–Lee Trevino

PUTTER POTPOURRI II

1. What golfing great came up with the term *yips* to describe the tension afflicting the nervous putter?

2. This golfing great invented the sand wedge in 1932. Name him.

3. What four events did Bobby Jones win when he captured the Grand Slam in 1930?

4. True or false? No American golfer made it to the final round of the 1959 British Open.

5. Who was the youngest golfer to win the U.S. Open?

6. If Tommy Aaron is first on the alphabetical list of players who have ever won a major, who's last?

7. In 1986, this golfer shot a final-round 63, but still finished second to Jack Nicklaus in The Masters. Who was it?

8. The oldest golf club in North America is located in what Canadian city?

9. Name the only two men to win the U.S. Amateur, U.S. Open and U.S. Senior Open in their careers.

10. Who finished second behind Tiger Woods at the 100th U.S. Open?

ANSWERS

1. Tommy Armour

2. Gene Sarazen

3. Jones won the U.S. Open, British Open, U.S. Amateur and the British Amateur.

4. True

5. Johnny McDermott was 19 years old when he won the title in 1911.

6. Fuzzy Zoeller, who won the 1979 Masters and the 1984 U.S. Open

7. Nick Price

8. Montreal — The Royal Montreal Golf Club was founded in 1873.

9. Arnold Palmer and Jack Nicklaus

10. Ernie Els and Miguel Angel Jiminez finished 15 strokes behind.

Chip Shots

"Golf is a game whose aim is to hit a very small ball into an even smaller hole, with weapons singularly ill-designed for that purpose."

–Winston Churchill

COMMON LINKS

Find the common link in each list below.

1. Prestwick in 1860, Newport in 1895, Siwanoy in 1916, Augusta in 1934

2. Jack Nicklaus in 1962, Jerry Pate in 1976, John Daly in 1991

3. Oakmont in 1962, Baltusrol in 1967, Pebble Beach in 1972, Baltusrol in 1980

4. Jerry Pate, Nick Price, Doug Weaver, Mark Wiebe

5. St. Andrews (NY), The Country Club, Shinnecock Hills, Newport, Chicago GC

6. Phil Mickelson, Bob Charles, Russ Cochran, Blaine McCallister

7. Carnoustie in 1975, Turnberry in 1977, Muirfield in 1980, Royal Troon in 1982, Royal Birkdale in 1983

8. Jock Hutchinson, Jim Barnes, Cyril Walker, Tommy Armour

9. Inwood in 1923, Scioto in 1926, Winged Foot in 1929, Interlachen in 1930

10. Tom Wargo, Larry Mowry, Simon Hobday, Larry Laoretti, Jim Albus

ANSWERS

1. The first course at which each of the professional majors was played

2. All three won major championships in their rookie year on the PGA Tour. Nicklaus and Pate won U.S. Opens, while Daly took the PGA title.

3. The courses at which Jack Nicklaus won his U.S. Opens

4. All four scored a hole-in-one on the par-3 sixth hole in the same round of the 1989 U.S. Open.

5. The five charter members of the USGA, which was founded in 1894

6. All four golfers putt left-handed.

7. The courses at which Tom Watson won his British Opens

8. These native-born Brits became naturalized American citizens by the time they won their majors in the 1920s and '30s.

9. The courses at which Bobby Jones won his U.S. Opens

10. All went winless on the PGA Tour, but won major championships on the Senior PGA Tour.

MISSING LINKS

Which one doesn't belong, and why?

1. Jack Nicklaus, Arnold Palmer, Raymond Floyd, Lee Trevino
2. Gary Player, Nick Faldo, Lee Trevino, Seve Ballesteros
3. Jerry Heard, Lee Trevino, Bobby Nichols, Bobby Clampett
4. Lou Graham, David Graham, Tom Watson, Andy North
5. Hale Irwin, Corey Pavin, T.C. Chen, Gil Morgan
6. Jack Nicklaus, Billy Casper, Johnny Miller, Hubert Green
7. Walter Hagen, Harry Vardon, Tom Watson, Gene Sarazen
8. Lanny Wadkins, Tom Lehman, Jay Haas, Curtis Strange
9. Chip Beck, Al Geiberger, Shigeki Maruyama, David Duval
10. Raymond Floyd, Tom Watson, Tom Kite, Tiger Woods

Chip Shots

"Some of us worship in churches, some in synagogues, some on golf courses."

–Adlai Stevenson

ANSWERS

1. Lee Trevino — He never won The Masters.

2. Lee Trevino — He won only two British Opens. The others have won three.

3. Bobby Clampett — He's never been, knock on wood, struck by lightning.

4. Andy North — The others have won one U.S. Open. North won two of them.

5. Corey Pavin — Pavin never lost a U.S. Open after leading after the first three rounds. The others, unfortunately, did.

6. Jack Nicklaus — He never won three straight PGA Tour events like the others.

7. Harry Vardon — He won six British Opens. The others didn't.

8. Tom Lehman — Lehman played college golf at Minnesota while the others matriculated at Wake Forest.

9. Shigeki Maruyama — He shot a 58 in the first round of qualifying for the 2000 U.S. Open. The others have recorded 59s on the PGA Tour.

10. Raymond Floyd — Floyd won his U.S. Open at Shinnecock Hills, while the other three won Opens at Pebble Beach.

QUOTE - UNQUOTE

Who said it? … and about whom?

1. "They always used to say the wind stopped for Hogan. Now it stops for [him]."

2. "I'm trying to win my own tournament. He's playing a different tournament. There's no way you're going to take that tournament."

3. "[He] has raised the bar, and it seems that he's the only guy who can jump over that bar."

4. "When he's putting the way he was this week, he's totally unbeatable."

5. "Whoever beats him has to play their best."

6. "For [him] to break par the way he has shows how he has separated himself not just from present-day golfers, but from golfers from the past, as well."

7. "It's kind of like Texas in the old Southwest Conference. You knew who was going to win before the game. It's certainly fun when you're pulling for Texas, but it's not real exciting for everybody else."

8. "It was like watching a Mercedes climb a hill. The power was there, the control was there. It's just on cruise control."

9. "It's just sometimes you're going to go through streaks where you're not going to play well. Hopefully, you can get through those periods of not playing well quickly."

10. "If you were building the complete golfer, you'd build [him]."

ANSWERS

1. Jack Nicklaus on Tiger Woods
2. Miguel Angel Jiminez on Tiger Woods
3. Tom Watson on Tiger Woods
4. John Huston on Tiger Woods
5. Fred Couples on Tiger Woods
6. Phil Mickelson on Tiger Woods
7. Former Longhorn Tom Kite on Tiger Woods
8. Earl Woods describing Tiger's 2000 U.S. Open victory
9. Tiger Woods on Tiger Woods
10. Mark O'Meara on Tiger Woods

CHIP SHOTS

"The perfect round of golf has never been played. It's 18 holes-in-one. I almost dreamt it once, but I lipped out at 18. I was mad as hell."

–*Ben Hogan*

GIVE ME
ANOTHER VOWEL

Here's a list of one-time British Open winners with the
vowels removed from their first and last names.
The order of the consonants has not been changed.
The year they won the title may help you out.

1. PLLWR, 1999

2. NBKRFNCH, 1991

3. MRKCLCVCCH, 1989

4. SNDYLYL, 1985

5. BLLRGRS, 1981

6. JHNNYMLLR, 1976

7. TNYJCKLN, 1969

8. RBRTDVCNZ, 1967

9. TNYLM, 1964

10. BNHGN, 1953

ANSWERS

1. Paul Lawrie
2. Ian Baker-Finch
3. Mark Calcavecchia
4. Sandy Lyle
5. Bill Rogers
6. Johnny Miller
7. Tony Jacklin
8. Roberto deVincenzo
9. Tony Lema
10. Ben Hogan

CHIP SHOTS

"I like golf because you can be really terrible at it and still not look much dorkier than anybody else."

–Humorist Dave Barry

SCORING IN THE '90s

How well do you remember golf in the 1990s?

1. When Tiger Woods cracked the $6 million mark in 1999, this golfer finished second in money earnings. Name him.

2. What two majors did Mark O'Meara win in 1998?

3. Of the ten U.S. Opens contested in the '90s, six of them were won by three golfers. Who are they?

4. How many of the four other Open winners of the decade can you name?

5. This golfer only needed five years to get 25 wins on the Senior PGA Tour, good for second place. Who was he?

6. Name the golfer who led the Seniors with 28 victories.

7. Two players with the same first name each won four majors in the '90s, tops on the PGA Tour. Who are they?

8. I went winless in two Ryder Cups, but was 3-0 in the 1993 Walker Cup as an amateur. Who am I?

9. Who won the most LPGA tournaments in the decade?

10. Tiger made the headlines, but this player made the money, topping the PGA Tour in earnings for the decade despite winning three fewer tournaments than Woods. Name him.

ANSWERS

1. David Duval won $3,641,906.

2. The Masters and the British Open

3. Payne Stewart, 1991 and '99; Lee Janzen, 1993 and '98; and Ernie Els, 1994 and '97

4. Hale Irwin, 1990; Tom Kite, 1992; Corey Pavin, 1995; and Steve Jones, 1996

5. Hale Irwin

6. Lee Trevino

7. Nick Price and Nick Faldo

8. Justin Leonard

9. Annika Sorenstam

10. Davis Love III earned a little more than $11.6 million. Tiger made over $11.3 million.

Chip Shots

"I'm waiting for the Senile Seniors Tour."

–Bob Hope, about his future in golf

THE PGA CHAMPIONSHIP

1. The 1958 championship was the first decided by stroke play, not match play. Who won it?

2. In 1924, he won the British Open and PGA Championship, a feat unmatched for seventy years. Who was he?

3. Who was the golfer who accomplished that same feat in 1994?

4. Name the oldest winner in the tournament's history.

5. Who are the only brothers to win the PGA?

6. True or false? Between 1950 and '70, no golfer won the event two years in a row.

7. Who won the first PGA Championship in 1916?

8. The 1977 tournament was the first major to be decided in a sudden-death playoff. Who was the winner?

9. Who won more PGA Championships, Walter Hagen or Jack Nicklaus?

10. Did Bobby Jones ever win the event in his career?

ANSWERS

1. Dow Finsterwald

2. Walter Hagen

3. Nick Price

4. Julius Boros was 48 years old when he won in 1968.

5. Lionel (1957) and Jay (1960) Herbert

6. True

7. Jim Barnes

8. Lanny Wadkins beat Gene Littler on the third hole of the playoff.

9. Both golfers won the tournament five times.

10. No

Chip Shots

"I told the caddie I wanted a sand wedge and he brought me a ham on rye."

–Chi Chi Rodriguez

OPEN SEASON

Match the British Open winner
with the course where he triumphed.

1. Ben Hogan, 1953
2. Greg Norman, 1993
3. Ian Baker-Finch, 1991
4. Seve Ballesteros, 1988
5. Tom Watson, 1982
6. Jack Nicklaus, 1978
7. Lee Trevino, 1972
8. Peter Thomson, 1956
9. Gene Sarazen, 1932
10. Harry Vardon, 1914

A) Royal Liverpool
B) Prince's, Kent
C) Royal St. George's
D) Carnoustie
E) Royal Latham
F) Prestwick
G) Royal Troon
H) Muirfield
I) Royal Birkdale
J) St. Andrews

CHIP SHOTS

"I used to play golf with a guy who cheated
so badly that he once had a hole-in-one and
wrote down zero on the scorecard."

–Bob Bruce

ANSWERS

1. D
2. C
3. I
4. E
5. G
6. J
7. H
8. A
9. B
10. F

CHIP SHOTS

"What's the penalty for killing a photographer — one stroke or two?"

-Davis Love III, after his swing was disturbed by a camera going off

BY THE NUMBERS

Do you know ...

1. The hole Gene Sarazen double-eagled in the 1935 Masters?

2. The number of men who have won the single-year Grand Slam?

3. Tiger Woods' margin of victory in the 2000 U.S. Open?

4. The number of women who have won the career LPGA Grand Slam?

5. Sam Snead's career PGA Tour victories?

6. The number of tournaments won by Byron Nelson in 1945?

7. The LPGA single-season record for wins?

8. Greg Norman's final round score when he won the 1986 British Open?

9. How many PGA Player of the Year awards Tom Watson won?

10. The number of players who have finished runner-up four times in a U.S. Open?

ANSWERS

1. The 15th hole

2. One — Bobby Jones in 1930

3. Fifteen strokes

4. Two — Pat Bradley and Juli Inkster have done it.

5. Eighty-one

6. Eighteen

7. Thirteen — Mickey Wright set it in 1963.

8. 63

9. Six

10. Four — Bobby Jones, Sam Snead, Arnold Palmer and Jack Nicklaus

Chip Shots

"I don't trust doctors. They are like golfers. Every one has a different answer to your problem."

–Seve Ballesteros

A FAMILY AFFAIR

1. His father pitched for four major league baseball teams while his uncle is in the Baseball Hall of Fame. He finished fifth on the money list in 1999. Who is this PGA Tour player?

2. These siblings each won a PGA Championship in their careers. Name them.

3. Name the pro who gets to call the 1968 Masters champion, "Uncle Bob."

4. Of seven brothers, Jim won the PGA Championship, Willie the U.S. Amateur, and Joe brought home fourteen Tour titles. What's the last name of this golfing family?

5. He's won over a million dollars on the Tour in his own right, but he will always be remembered as the son of "Mr. 59." Name this father-son duo.

6. Lloyd won thirty-six times, including the 1946 U.S. Open. His brother, Ray, had five victories. Can you think of their last name?

7. His eight PGA Tour wins were seventy-three less than his Uncle Sam's. Who is he?

8. This father-son combo won eight British Opens between them, including four in a row by the son. Name them.

9. In 1999, he produced the best final round in PGA Tour history, firing a 59 to win the Bob Hope Chrysler Classic. His father almost matched him with a 61 at the Emerald Coast Classic on the Senior Tour. Who's the son?

10. Alex and Willie won U.S. Opens, but brother Macdonald had twenty-four career wins. The only common thing about these brothers is their last name. What is it?

ANSWERS

1. Chris Perry

2. Lionel and Jay Herbert

3. Jay Haas is the nephew of Bob Goalby.

4. Turnesa

5. Al and Brent Geiberger

6. Mangrum

7. J.C. Snead, nephew of Sam Snead

8. Tom Morris, Sr. and Jr.

9. David Duval — His father is Senior PGA Tour player, Bob Duval.

10. Smith

Chip shots

"They call it golf because all the other four-letter words were taken."

–Raymond Floyd

INITIALLY SPEAKING

Identify each golfer from the initials and clues.

1. T.K. — Won the 1992 U.S. Open at the age of 42

2. J.S. — The first woman golf pro to design golf courses

3. M.B. — Dubbed "Mr. X" because of his fondness for solitude

4. P.T. — Five-time winner of the British Open

5. H.R. — First winner of the U.S. Open

6. S.G. — Shot a 62 in his first round as a pro on the PGA Tour

7. C.S. — Last golfer to win back-to-back U.S. Opens

8. P.M. — 1999 was the first winless season of his career

9. K.W. — Came from eight strokes back to win the 1999 duMaurier Classic, her first major

10. H.I. — Oldest winner of the U.S. Open

ANSWERS

1. Tom Kite
2. Jan Stephenson
3. Miller Barber
4. Peter Thomson
5. Horace Rawlins
6. Sergio Garcia
7. Curtis Strange
8. Phil Mickelson
9. Karrie Webb
10. Hale Irwin

Chip Shots

"The reason the pro tells you to keep your head down is so you can't see him laughing."

–Comedienne Phyllis Diller

TRUE OR FALSE?

1. No golfer named Joe won a major championship in the 1900s.

2. In 1994, Fuzzy Zoeller earned more than one million dollars, but didn't win a tournament.

3. No Irishman has ever won a major championship.

4. The first time total prize money at a U.S. Open exceeded $1,000 was in 1931.

5. Hal Sutton's only major tournament win was at the 1983 Masters.

6. Ben Hogan was given a ticker-tape parade up Broadway when he returned home after winning the 1953 British Open.

7. Jack Nicklaus was the first golfer to earn more than two million dollars in his career.

8. The course at the Olympic Club in San Francisco has no water hazards.

9. No amateur has won the U.S. Open since Bobby Jones retired in 1930.

10. President Grover Cleveland decided against taking up golf in retirement because he was too fat.

ANSWERS

1. True

2. True — Zoeller had five runner-up finishes.

3. False — Ireland's Fred Daly won the 1947 British Open by one stroke.

4. False — The first time was in 1916.

5. False — His only major win was in the 1983 PGA Championship.

6. True — It was the first for an American golfer since Bobby Jones in 1930.

7. True

8. True

9. False — Amateur John Goodman won it in 1933.

10. True

CHIP SHOTS

"Now I can see I can't make anything."

–Jack Nicklaus, on his new contact lenses

WHO AM I?

1. Jack Nicklaus was making a bid for the Grand Slam in 1972 until I put an end to it with a win in the British Open.

2. In my first major in the United States as a pro, I finished second at the 1999 PGA Championship at the age of nineteen.

3. I was the first president of the Augusta National GC.

4. I was the only golfer to win the U.S. Open twice during the 1970s.

5. I tied the record when I shot a 59 at the 1991 Las Vegas International.

6. I'm the last golfer to win three tournaments in a row. The year was 1978.

7. I got my nickname when I told the press I would set them up with champagne instead of beer if I won the 1962 Orange County Open.

8. My chip-in on the 17th at Pebble Beach enabled me to beat Jack Nicklaus in the 1982 U.S. Open.

9. I was the leading money winner on the LPGA Tour a record eight times.

10. I competed in twenty-two U.S. Opens before winning the title in 1986.

ANSWERS

1. Lee Trevino
2. Sergio Garcia
3. Bobby Jones
4. Hale Irwin
5. Chip Beck
6. Gary Player
7. "Champagne" Tony Lema
8. Tom Watson
9. Kathy Whitworth
10. Raymond Floyd

CHIP SHOTS

"I hit two fairways — well, maybe four, but only two I was aiming at."

-John Daly

LADIES' CHOICE AGAIN

1. Who's the LPGA Hall of Famer who graduated Phi Beta Kappa from the University of Texas with a degree in physics?

2. Mickey Wright was the first golfer to defend her U.S. Women's Open title. Who was second?

3. True or false? LPGA star Laura Davies once won a long-drive competition by out-hitting forty men with a drive of 312 yards.

4. This Swedish golfer's first victory on the Tour was at the 1988 Open on her way to being named Rookie of the Year. What's her name?

5. Name the South Carolina college that LPGA players Betsy King, Beth Daniel and Dottie Mochrie attended.

6. The lowest round in U.S. Women's Open history is a 65 by this South African golfer. Who is she?

7. Who holds the LPGA record of four victories at the LPGA Championship?

8. What's the name of the competition between the professional golfers of the United States and Europe?

9. In 1987, this golfer became the first British woman to win the U.S. Women's Open. Name her.

10. Three players in LPGA history have won back-to-back LPGA Championships. How many can you name?

ANSWERS

1. Betsy Rawls

2. Donna Caponi won the title in 1969 and '70.

3. True

4. Liselotte Neumann

5. Furman University

6. Sally Little — Ironically, it's the only major she's never won.

7. Mickey Wright, in 1958, '60, '61, and '63

8. The Solheim Cup

9. Laura Davies

10. Mickey Wright, 1960 and '61; Patty Sheehan, 1983 and '84; and Juli Inkster, 1999 and 2000

Chip Shots

"You've just one problem. You stand too close to the ball — after you've hit it."

–Sam Snead, to a pupil

THE BACK NINE

1. Tom Weiskopf's win at the 1973 British Open was the only major championship of his PGA career. On what course did he win the event?

2. The first time galleries were kept off the fairways and behind ropes was at the 1954 U.S. Open. Where was it held?

3. The three-hole stretch from the 11th to 13th holes at Augusta National is known by what nickname?

4. What's the name of the country club which hosted the first PGA Championship in 1916?

5. True or false? The famous Old course at St. Andrews is owned by the Church of St. Andrew in Scotland.

6. At what course did Walter Hagen win his fourth straight PGA Championship, a record still unmatched?

7. The longest par-3 hole on the PGA Tour is the 246-yard 13th at this club's Blue Course. Name the club.

8. In 1968, Lee Trevino became the first golfer in U.S. Open history to shoot less than seventy in all four rounds. Where did he do it?

9. At 7,252 yards, it's the longest course ever played in British Open competition. Name it.

10. Buy yourself a beverage of your choice at the nineteenth hole if you can name the club where the PGA Championship was held for the first time in California. The year was 1929.

ANSWERS

1. Royal Troon, Scotland

2. Baltusrol GC, New Jersey

3. Amen Corner

4. Siwanoy CC, New York

5. False — It's a public course owned by the City of St. Andrews, Scotland.

6. It happened in 1927 at Cedar Crest in Dallas, Texas.

7. The Doral CC, Florida

8. Oak Hill CC, Minnesota

9. Carnoustie, Scotland

10. Hillcrest CC, Los Angeles — Buy yourself another one if you said Leo Diegel was the winner.

Chip Shots

"Belly dancers would make great golfers. They never move their heads."

–*Phil Rodgers*

COMING IN

1. What's the biggest possible margin in eighteen holes of match play?

2. Golf made its national TV debut with the final round of the World Championship of Golf in:
   a) 1951 b) 1953 c) 1955 d) 1957

3. I joined the PGA Tour in 1987 and had at least one win in each of my first seven years, including the 1993 PGA Championship. Who am I?

4. Who holds the record for the longest time between victories at The Masters?

5. Who was the first French golfer to play for the European team in a Ryder Cup?

6. When was the last time a golfer won the U.S. Open in his first attempt?

7. Five Americans have won the British Open in consecutive years. How many can you name?

8. Who holds the PGA record for career holes-in-one?

9. The U.S. Open, first held in 1895, is the oldest tournament on the PGA Tour. What event is the second oldest?

10. What do you call a golfer with a zero handicap, besides good?

ANSWERS

1. 10 and 8

2. B

3. Paul Azinger

4. Jack Nicklaus — Nicklaus first won the tournament in 1963 and then again in 1986, a span of 23 years.

5. Jean Van de Velde, in 1999

6. 1913, when Francis Ouimet won the championship

7. Bobby Jones, 1926 and '27; Walter Hagen, 1928 and '29; Arnold Palmer, 1961 and '62; Lee Trevino, 1971 and '72; Tom Watson, 1982 and '83

8. Art Wall, Jr. — Wall aced 37 holes in his career.

9. The Western Open, first contested in 1899

10. Green with envy, you would call him a scratch golfer.

CHIP SHOTS

"I couldn't read the break in the green from the tee."

-Gary Player, after just missing a hole-in-one